TAME TURTLE

 Connect the dots from **1** to **5**.
Color the picture.

Dot-to-Dots

Connect the dots from **1** to **5**.
Color the picture.

Dot-to-Dots

BEE BOP

Connect the dots from 1 to 10.
Color the picture.

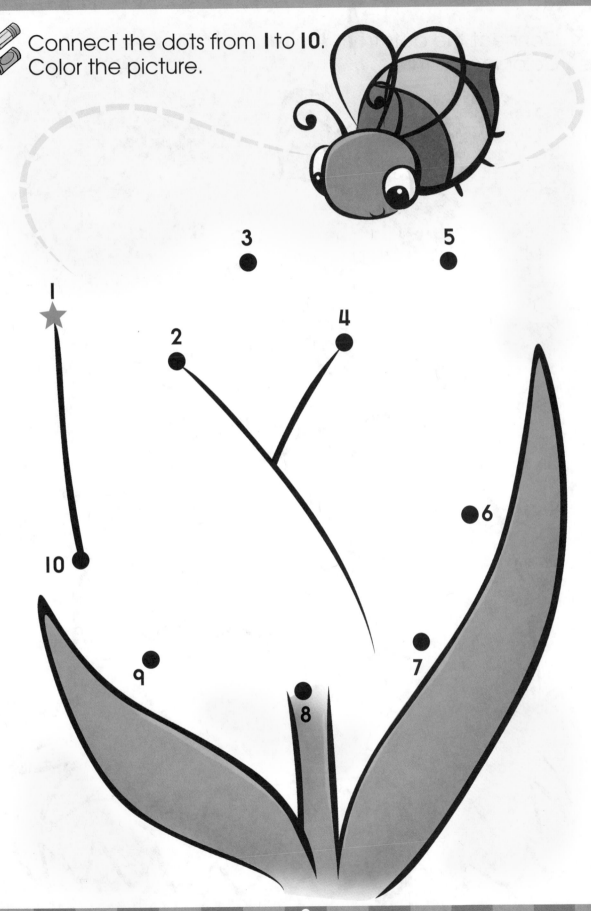

Dot-to-Dots

Connect the dots from **1** to **10**.
Color the picture.

Dot-to-Dots   ©School Zone Publishing Company 02190

Connect the dots from **I** to **20**.
Color the picture.

©School Zone Publishing Company 02190

Dot-to-Dots

PRANCING PENGUIN

 Connect the dots from **1** to **20**.
 Color the picture.

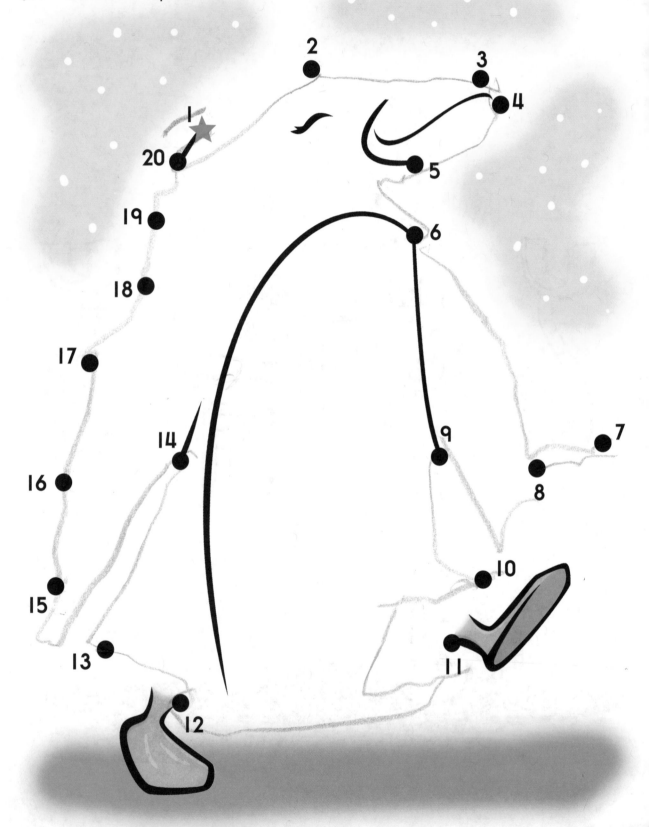

Dot-to-Dots   ©School Zone Publishing Company 02190

SETTING SAIL

 Connect the dots from **1** to **25**.
Color the picture.

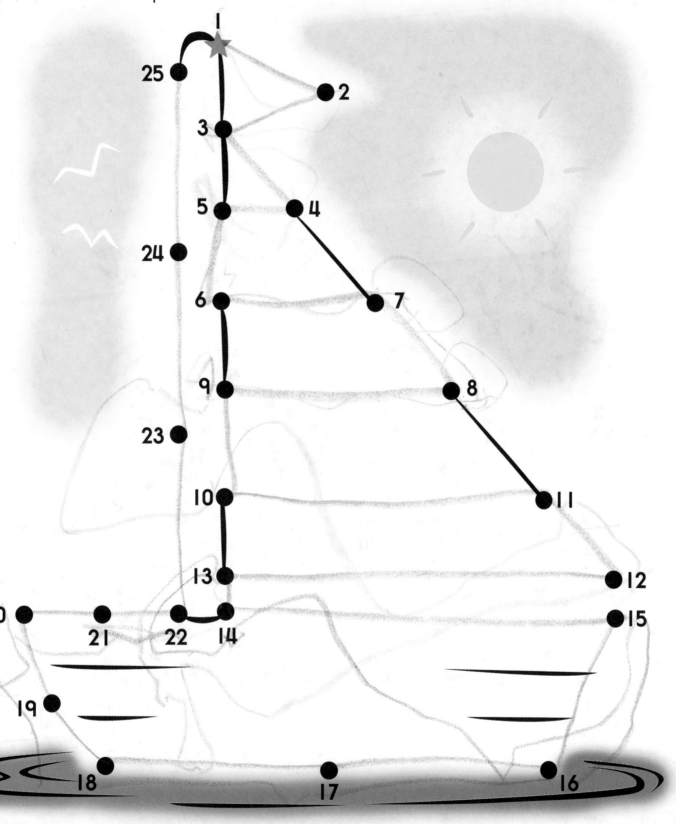

Dot-to-Dots

Connect the dots from **1** to **25**.
Color the picture.

Connect the dots from **1** to **25**.
Color the picture.

Dot-to-Dots

Connect the dots from **1** to **25**.
Color the picture.

Connect the dots from **1** to **25**.
Color the picture.

Dot-to-Dots

SOMETHING FISHY

 Connect the dots from 1 to 25.
Color the picture.

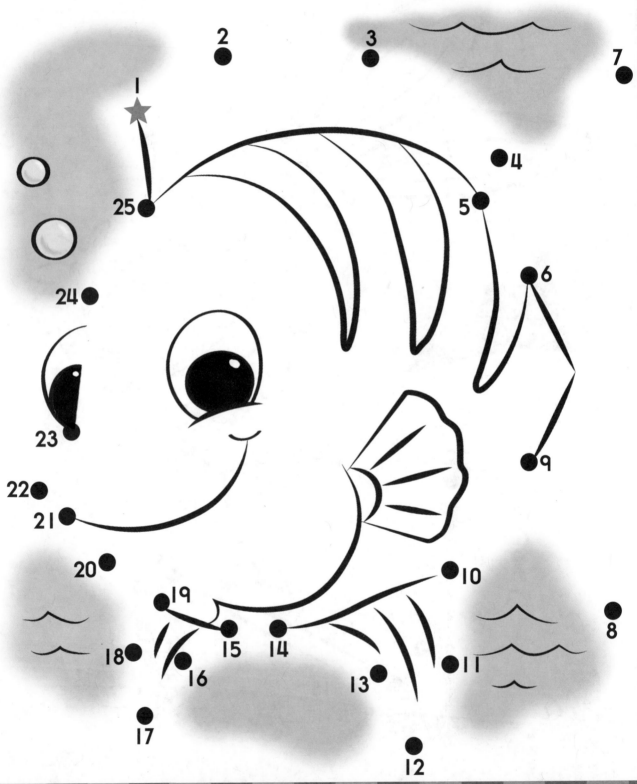

Dot-to-Dots Numbers 02190